CONFIDENCE-BOOSTING

for staging a music

THE SHOW MUST GO ON!

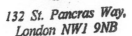

132 St. Pancras Way,
London NW1 9NB

Tel: 020-7482-5424
Fax: 020-7482-5434
E-mail: dot@dotsonline.co.uk
Web: www.dotsonline.co.uk

Lin Marsh & Wendy Cook

FABER *ff* MUSIC

6·25

Lin Marsh

Lin is well known as an inspirational force both within the classroom and on the stage. As well as directing Oxfordshire Youth Music Theatre, she is a vocal coach and workshop leader for National Youth Music Theatre. Lin and Wendy have already collaborated in the writing of the musical *Torchbearers*, which reached the finals for the Vivian Ellis Awards in 2000.

Wendy Cook

Wendy has directed and choreographed shows in venues both in this country and abroad. She works with many different organizations including the NYMT, the London Mozart Players and Merseyside Youth Arts, and frequently works closely with Lin leading music-theatre workshops for young people and teachers.

The authors are very grateful to the following for their invaluable help in the writing of this book: Caroline Astell-Burt, Bruce Pullan, Mary King, Sheila Russell, Val Whitlock, Syd Ralph, Judy Tompsett and Julie Greenfield.

© 2001 by Faber Music Ltd
First published in 2001 by Faber Music Ltd
3 Queen Square London WC1N 3AU
Illustrations by Harry Venning
Design by Nick Flower
Printed in England by Caligraving Ltd

ISBN 0-571-52102-9

To buy Faber Music publications or to find out about the full range of titles available please contact your local music retailer or Faber Music sales enquiries:

Faber Music Limited, Burnt Mill,
Elizabeth Way, Harlow, CM20 2HX England
Tel: +44 (0)1279 82 89 82
Fax: +44 (0)1279 82 89 83
sales@fabermusic.com
www.fabermusic.com

Contents

Introduction

The musical is one of the most enjoyable and accessible of theatrical experiences, for performers and audience alike. Every school puts on a show, every town has an amateur operatic or musical society, and taking part in such performances often remains a highlight in the memory.

It is important to remember that people can achieve just as high vocal standards in musicals as they can in opera or choral singing; at all times it is the quality of the singing, acting and movement that should be paramount. Those who take part in musical theatre productions are usually confident in one particular skill—singing, acting or dancing—but quickly find that they have to draw on all performing skills, familiar and unfamiliar. This, although challenging and exciting, can also be frightening!

The show must go on! offers practical strategies to ensure that your show runs smoothly and successfully. Although there is no definitive way to put on a show, our suggestions are based on many years of working with all age groups in a variety of settings; from classroom or village hall to fully professional theatres. Despite the inevitable technical hiccups and the constant cry of "if only we had more ... money, time, space, tenors!", we have had great fun and continue to be amazed and thrilled by performance standards, often achieved against the odds. We hope this book will be useful to you as a starting point if embarking upon your first venture in music theatre, or as a source of new ideas if you are an old hand.

Although challenging and exciting, performance can also be frightening

General principles

Music theatre is a collaborative process; the artistic and technical teams need to work together as closely as the company of performers. A full-scale production is a huge undertaking and the workload often falls heavily on the shoulders of a small number of committed people. This way madness lies! It is far better to spread the net wider, drawing on the skills and experience of others. In schools or amateur societies some production roles may be combined, so a director might also design or choreograph, but ultimately one person will need to take responsibility for each of the roles outlined below.

Regular production meetings will ensure that the team talks to each other, that deadlines are agreed, that problems are spotted early and budgets not exceeded. If you set an agenda early on and stick to it, colleagues will be more likely to attend. Make sure any decisions are relayed to absentees, as there is nothing worse than hearing: "But no one told me!" Book the hall for regular rehearsals and the performance week as soon as possible, making sure that the dates don't clash with examinations, parents' evenings or the local W.I. dinner!

Once you have decided which show to tackle (see *Choosing repertoire*, page 12), start to talk about it with great enthusiasm to as many people as you can. The excitement you generate will spur others to action; don't underestimate the energy required to inspire interest and commitment.

Director

The buck stops here! The Director is ultimately responsible for ensuring that everything runs as smoothly as possible. She/he is responsible for:

❖ Getting to know the show before rehearsals start.
❖ Researching the show and its background through books, videos, film, visual art and so on. There are some excellent specialist libraries and collections such as Cecil Sharp House, the Theatre Museum, the Fan Museum, and many others that offer wonderful resources.
❖ Artistic direction, i.e. the way the show is presented: is it to be done in its own period, or will it be a modern-dress version? Is the interpretation conventional or radical, sumptuous or minimalist? It is the Director's vision that informs all aspects of the artistic input to the show.
❖ Briefing, then consulting and liaising with the Designer(s), Choreographer and Musical Director; from the 'ideas' stage to the final performance.

- ❖ Working closely with the Stage Manager and backstage crew, ensuring that all props are being sought and that budgets are being drawn up and adhered to.
- ❖ Drawing up a production schedule (see page 38) and ensuring that it is publicized and implemented.
- ❖ Putting together and distributing a rehearsal schedule (see page 36) which is the blueprint for progression to performance.
- ❖ Ensuring that budgets are realistic and setting up budgetary control mechanisms.

Choreographer

The responsibilities of the Choreographer will vary considerably from show to show, as different directors require different amounts of input. In terms of style and interpretation however, it is important that everyone pulls in the same direction. The Musical Director is a very important friend to have! She/he will be able to help analyse the music and make rehearsal tapes. Preparation needs to be thorough, both of the music and the text, so that you know the plot line and understand how the choreography fits into the show as a whole.

Costume can be a major problem if you haven't had early, friendly discussions with the Costume Designer or Wardrobe Master/Mistress. After you have expressed your appreciation of the general design, here are some issues you might want to raise:

- ❖ Can the performers lift up their arms without the whole costume rising to neck level?
- ❖ Those skirts will have a split in the side, won't they?
- ❖ Does it have to be white? (Dancers hate white; it makes them look 'huge', and that's quite apart from laundering problems.)
- ❖ How are they going to keep those hats on without constant fiddling?

Musical Director (M.D.)

The Musical Director is responsible for:

- ❖ Teaching the songs.
- ❖ Organizing the band.
- ❖ Accompanying at rehearsals.
- ❖ Conducting the show.

She/he must ensure that band parts are booked in good time and decide how many players are needed, as sometimes there is a choice of orchestration. Decisions will also have to be made about whether to involve young players.

For example, inexperienced wind players often cannot play very quietly, which makes it hard work for young voices.

Orchestral stands will need lights and these can be hired for the week of the show. If you have your own, make sure they work and that you have spare bulbs. Never underestimate the number of extension leads and four-way sockets you will need!

If a sound system is going to be used, the M.D. will need to find a Sound Engineer (a teacher, senior pupil or a professional firm). If radio microphones are used, the sound needs plotting (organizing) and performers will need to work with them in good time before the show opens. Very often, changes of battery packs require practice in rehearsal. This can be done before the hired microphones are available, by attaching a piece of cord or thick string to a numbered disc and passing it between those who are sharing.

It is very helpful if the M.D. prepares a working audio tape for the Choreographer, after having agreed any cuts in the music. Dance sections are frequently too long for 'non-dancers' or can be too short to accommodate the action indicated in the script, and should be cut or expanded to suit. Commercial recordings of musicals are notoriously different from the printed score, so never rely on them for choreography! A Musical Director has to know the music thoroughly and agree the tempi (speeds) with the Choreographer. This is often a compromise between the speed the band can manage, the speed that the performers can dance, and the directions in the score. Young singers cannot sustain long phrases when the tempo is slow and tend to sing flat; too fast and the chorus words are lost and the dancers fall flat on their faces!

Dance sections are frequently too long for 'non-dancers'

If you can find a willing and competent répétiteur (rehearsal pianist), you can double up on rehearsal time by having one person working with the Choreographer and one for solo or chorus work. As musical work is so noisy, it is useful to have at least two separate working spaces.

Designer

The Designer has to start work right at the beginning of the whole process and work very closely with the Director. She/he is responsible for:

- Deciding where the best place for the audience is, so they can all see the performers.
- Devising the best shape stage, i.e. using blocks or rostra to build up the floor so that all the performers can be seen clearly.
- Solving problems with the Director, whose ideas on staging are often very imaginative but not necessarily practical.
- Listening to the Choreographer when she/he says that forty-five people dancing a wild bacchanalia will need more than three square metres of space!
- Suggesting the use of unusual props, masks or puppets in the show.
- Designing costumes which complement the interpretative ideas of the Director and Choreographer, but which are practical and possible in terms of resources and funding.
- Styling the show, particularly in relation to costume, make-up and hair. Style can be achieved by means of simple but authentic details. For example, the cast for a show set in the 1920s (such as *Anything Goes*) could be given typical hairstyles of the period, emphasizing the energy of young women of that time. Dramatic make-up would also be appropriate.
- Minimal make-up, used only to enhance the features under strong lighting, can also be effective in creating a more naturalistic style. Special effects make-up can offer scope for face-painting projects with children. Character make-up is best left to a specialist, especially when trying to age a young face.

Wardrobe Master/Mistress

Even if the costumes are simple, there is always a huge amount of organization needed. It is useful to have someone who doesn't panic, doesn't take offence and can work quickly under pressure! She/he must be capable of:

- Planning and making the costumes.
- Deciding what the performers can bring in themselves and giving clear instructions to them.
- Deciding what needs to be made, hired or borrowed.
- Ensuring that everything is labelled.
- Making 'add-ons' that contribute to the style of the costumes, such as sashes, hats or armour.

* Keeping, checking and repairing costumes during the performance period.
* Achieving uniformity where it is required, for example, through consistent skirt lengths.

It may be that a decision is made to hire a whole set of show costumes. It can be an expensive option and sometimes the term 'set ' is used very loosely. It is probably best to ask around to find a good supplier.

Lighting Designer

This is also a designing job and its extent is dependent on budget and the resources of your venue. It could be that the show is performed in daylight. If not, you will need to liaise with someone who knows about electricity and safety. Responsibilities include:

* Understanding the various moods of the piece.
* Liaising with the Director to establish how the scenes are set, and who and what needs lighting.
* Checking the available lighting equipment and noting what may need to be hired.
* Planning special effects such as overhead projectors, slide projectors, torches, dimmers or even Christmas tree lights.

Operating lights for a show is a very attractive activity for computer addicts and those keen to put their knowledge of physics into practice. Without wishing to dampen their enthusiasm, it is really important that a firm hand is kept on their activities because the chances are they will know very little about theatre and stage lighting.

Stage Manager (S.M.)

The Stage Manager takes charge when the show is running and has a complete grasp of the piece regarding lighting changes, effects cues, scenery changes, and cast entrances and exits. As soon as rehearsals begin, she/he is responsible for:

* Measuring and marking the floor space so everyone knows where to go (particularly important if the rehearsal and performance venues are not one and the same).
* Collecting, storing and marking all props and furniture needed for the show.
* The placing of characters or groups, entrances and exits, scene changes, positioning of furniture, use of props and special effects (lighting and sound if used); these should be plotted and noted in 'the book'.

- Making the stage area safe and clean for the performers.
- Informing the company when to be ready to go on stage.
- Cueing sound effects, lighting and scenery movement.
- Health and safety in the rehearsal space and on stage (see *Boring, but essential!*, page 45).

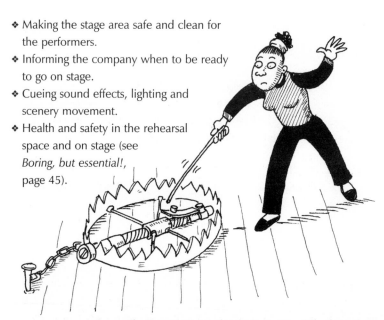

The Stage Manager makes the stage area safe for the performers

Publicity Officer

Marketing a show and ensuring it is publicized in the right places is a time-consuming and frustrating process. The main skills required are persistence and confidence. You need to have faith that your show is going to be a success and not be shy about brandishing flyers and posters whenever the opportunity arises. Your responsibilities are as follows:

- Organizing the printing and distribution of posters and flyers (liaise with the Designer to ensure all relevant information is on the poster, including special wording agreed with the licensee).
- Finding out how many people you can legally seat in the venue and printing tickets.
- Arranging publicity photographs shortly before the performance.
- Contacting the local press/radio/television.
- Making contact directly with local schools, community groups and amateur theatre groups.
- Inviting V.I.P.s to the production and welcoming them on the night.

Front of House

Dealing with a different audience for each performance is a complicated and important task. With your helpers, your job is to make them feel welcome, comfortable and safe. Plan the team carefully so all areas are covered, and agree on a particular code of dress so that you can be identified by the public. Your responsibilities include:

* Arriving early to ensure the auditorium and cloakrooms are clean (liaise with the caretaker/cleaners).
* Checking that there are clear signs to fire exits, car-parking facilities, refreshment areas and cloakrooms.
* Ensuring there is a suitable space for wheelchair users, and that all exits are unobstructed.
* Organizing programme-sellers and providing a float for them and the box office.
* Finding out how many seats are sold before each performance (liaise with the box office) and selling any remaining tickets.
* Showing people to their seats. This includes knowing where to seat complimentary ticket holders, and who they are!
* Signalling the end of the interval (liaise with the Director) and collecting lost property at the end.
* Asking the audience to turn off all mobile phones and informing them of the agreed policy on photography and videotaping during the show. Flash photography in particular can be a real problem: it is distracting for cast and other audience members alike. Be aware that videotaping the show could also be an infringement of copyright.

Production Manager

The Production Manager coordinates the various aspects of the whole production, from the start of discussions to the final get-out. She/he runs the early planning meetings before work starts on the production so that a detailed budget can be drawn up and controlled. Keeping a show within its financial means can entail saying 'no' to a director who has declared that the success of the show depends upon the appearance of a giant frog with eyes that light up! Such last minute whims might seem a very small thing for a director or designer, but have important financial implications.

Time management is crucial. If the Set Designer wanted to paint the stage floor just before the dress rehearsal, it would be the Production Manager's responsibility to re-schedule the painting. If a chime at a particular pitch for a church bell effect is deemed essential, or the lorry delivering the scaffolding is late or lost; the Production Manager must solve the problem!

2 Choosing repertoire

If putting on a musical is an annual event, the search for next year's show begins as soon as the curtain goes down for the last performance. There seems to be a very small list of musicals performed year after year by schools and youth groups; they are tried and tested and guaranteed to attract an audience, but often may not be suitable for the age range, vocal range or gender mix in the potential cast. Let us consider what makes a good choice.

Age range

For a cast of any age, the story must be comprehensible and in some way relevant to them. Pupils in primary school cannot be expected to play out love stories or act the part of a father losing his three daughters (*Fiddler on the Roof*) with any understanding or credibility. Instead, look for material that will capture the imagination; there are wonderful myths and legends that have been set to music, also contemporary stories relating to the environment or technology. It is sad to hear of primary schools performing *Grease* when they have not explored musicals that have more appropriate content. There are also many musicals aimed even at infant level, so choosing a good one should not be a problem. Do consider very carefully the words, number of verses, vocal range and plot relevance. For example:

- ❖ Are the melodies attractive with good word-setting?
- ❖ Is the theme or story suitable?
- ❖ Is there any opportunity for movement?
- ❖ Can the dialogue be spread between several children?
- ❖ Is it a suitable length for young children?
- ❖ Is the piano part playable by one of the staff or does it come with a CD/tape?

Age range: is the theme or story suitable?

It is well worth looking at dramatic cantatas (see *Appendix*, page 47) and considering how they might be used as the basis for a music-theatre piece. If the theme or story is varied enough, there will be opportunities for pupils' composition, poetry, dialogue and movement to expand the piece into a much larger production, using the songs as a link. That aside, there is a plethora of material sitting on shelves in music shops and in glossy, colourful catalogues especially for the junior/middle school age range (8–12).

Secondary schools and operatic societies are able to tackle more weighty issues and many perform musicals from the mainstream repertoire. However, a piece which has a strong love element (such as *Carousel* or *South Pacific*) requires mature acting and it is often difficult to bring off a production when a pupil of fourteen may be playing a forty year-old. Similarly, companies with predominantly mature members are unlikely to take on *Fame* when they can deliver *The Mikado* or *Chess* far more convincingly.

Some musicals written for schools have tried to address social or historical events and unfortunately seem rather worthy as a result. Others have set out to be comedies but the jokes become dated and the pupils quickly tire of them. Consider the following:

- ❖ Is the story line strong and interesting?
- ❖ Will it be appropriate for your pupils/audience/venue?
- ❖ Do the songs have good lyrics/interesting melodies/contrasting dramatic styles?
- ❖ Are there enough parts for principals?
- ❖ Is there plenty for the chorus to do?
- ❖ Does the dialogue flow easily?

Vocal range

Singing has sadly declined in secondary classrooms and therefore in the population at large, though pupils are still keen to sing pop/rock music and to take part in musicals. Role models in the pop world have not always helped inform the making of a good sound however, and this has lead to the overuse of microphones and the underuse of good breath support. Conventional musicals from the 1940s and '50s were written with trained singers in mind so, to compensate, try these strategies to find your way around extreme vocal ranges:

- ❖ It is not practical to transpose choruses but it is possible to re-arrange the parts to make use of your more competent singers.

- ❖ Do not strain young male voices. Avoid extreme low or high notes by changing the octave, dropping or raising to harmonize, or even speaking the part in places if it is a dramatic song.
- ❖ Make sure lyrics are used clearly so that the voice itself is not forced.
- ❖ Work with female singers so they understand when to use chest register in a song and when they must move into head voice to avoid strain and harshness in the sound (see *Register*, page 32).

Practical resources

We have seen school productions performed on stages, in amphitheatres, in churches and in professional theatres. There are no rules as to what works; it falls to the Director and Designer to make the best use of the available space and budget. Often, the very lack of facilities makes for creative and imaginative theatre! However, take a long, hard look at the stage and auditorium available to you and be realistic about what you and your team can undertake. A dramatic performance invites the audience to suspend disbelief, so large painted backdrops and cumbersome scenery are not necessarily the key to success.

Essential questions to address before you make a decision are:

- ❖ Can the stage or performance space accommodate all the performers needed in the most populated scene?
- ❖ Is the wing space adequate for storing set/ props and for performers waiting to make an entrance?

❖ How many entrances to the performance space are there? Are there any treads to enable access from the auditorium to the stage?

If you are considering a show that requires a lot of dance or choreographed movement and you have a pianist with limited ability, this will obviously affect the choice of music: it is probably not a good idea to attempt any Sondheim! Alternatively, consider finding a rehearsal and/or performance accompanist (répétiteur).

Devising your own piece

Devising your own piece around a particular theme or story fills many artistic teams with apprehension. However, it can be an excellent way of tailoring material to suit the needs, interests and skills of your group. Many inventive ideas can be drawn from the performers themselves, who can be particularly good at finding practical solutions to directorial or choreographic problems. Putting ideas into the melting pot, trying them out and making them work is a satisfying experience, but do bear the following points in mind:

❖ It would be unwise to attempt a full-length devised work on a first go. Instead, try twenty to thirty minutes.
❖ Simplify the plot to its bare bones.
❖ Keep moves on and off stage to a minimum; if space allows, try having the cast on stage throughout the piece, using their bodies or voices to support the main action.
❖ Minimize the dialogue to maximize the action and singing.
❖ Find a clear visual style to unify the presentation.
❖ Ask for songs of no more than three to four minutes in length, with plenty of variety and good potential for physical/theatrical action.

Find a starting point: a story or theme to provide a structure around which to work. Ask a composer (well ahead of the start of the devising rehearsals) to write between four and six main songs. If you don't have access to the services of a composer, then look at existing cantatas. These are collections of songs composed around particular themes, such as Ocean World by Peter Rose and Anne Conlon (see Appendix, page 47). Devise dramatic or choreographed action around the songs, or create opportunities for the pupils to perform their own compositions.

Opportunities to develop dance or movement often emerge in the transitions or links between songs. In devising music theatre, these spaces can be used to:

- ❖ Create continuity; maintaining pace, flow and performers' concentration.
- ❖ Develop choreographic ideas within the lyrics or music of the songs.
- ❖ Develop dramatic or narrative elements, dialogue, characters or story-telling.
- ❖ Explore the use of objects such as large pieces of cloth, rope, umbrellas, body extensions (elongating the arms with cloth and sticks), masks, fans, large-scale puppets or streamers to increase the theatricality of the piece.

The benefits of devising soon become apparent, primarily as ensemble performance comes to the fore, but also because you can create opportunities to allow particular individuals to shine.

The artistic team will have done a great deal of preparatory work before beginning rehearsals. Remember that the cast can't read your mind however, so it is a good idea to share this information, using a variety of different approaches to instil enthusiasm and interest them in the story.

Games

There are lots of games designed to break the ice, free people's bodies and imaginations, develop group feeling and so on. A word of warning: make sure the mechanics, progression and organization of any game are fully grasped before introducing it to the group. Having it fall apart at the seams is a bit like telling a joke and forgetting the end!

Story-telling

Ask the cast to give a verbal synopsis of the story by designing tableaux (still group pictures or photographs) that illustrate interesting moments in the drama. Everyone has to be involved: they could be furniture, pumpkins or sundry animals, as required. Make sure there is a good mix of age/gender in each group, as a group of under-twelves will take for ever to agree a common strategy and come up with the goods. Ask them to design four tableaux and then present them to the rest of the group in the order in which they occur in the story. The others can play 'Guess the moment', and fill in the events between each tableau. All the groups can then improvise dramatic action and dialogue using one tableau as a starting point.

Character work

Ask each member of the cast to invent a history for one of the characters in the story: age, family background, attitude and relationship to other characters, social class or status, previous history and so on. Working in twos, each tell the other about their character and encourage the listener to ask questions which must be answered in role; perhaps set it up as a radio or TV interview. Alternatively, introduce a 'hot seat' where one character is asked searching questions by the rest of the group. If an ensemble performer hasn't got a character name, encourage them to invent one and justify their choice. This technique could be employed when characters are allocated. Naturalistic shows such as *Fiddler on the Roof* or *West Side Story* benefit from this type of practical preparation work. Shows such as *A Funny Thing Happened on the Way to the Forum* or *Annie* require a more stylized approach to creating character through immediate (almost cartoon-like) physicality. Play with such characteristics as wily, nervous, brash, humble, proud, shifty, wilful and so on.

Context

If the show is set in another time or place, provide background information to help the performers develop an understanding of its context. For example, to a young cast, *Chess* could be incomprehensible unless there is at least a basic understanding of the Cold War. This kind of information can be imparted in a number of ways including improvisations based on specific incidents, or newspaper photographs and reports from the time.

Style

Identify the essential ingredients of the particular style. Look at the fashions for women and men, as clothes and accessories affect how a person moves. If everybody wore hats, ask Wardrobe if you can have a set of hats to use at this early stage. Listen to music from the period; is it flamboyant or delicate, precise or impressionistic? Run a social dance workshop that includes some exploration of etiquette, such as bows and curtseys. What was the prevailing mood of the time?

Read-through

A read-through can be useful to the cast by helping them to have a rudimentary idea of the piece as a whole (although this would not be appropriate with a group of very young performers). If there are younger ones or people with reading difficulties in your cast, make sure they are sitting next to someone sympathetic who can help them. It's important to ring the changes in the reading, so swap large parts around. The read-through is not very useful for deciding who would play a particular part well; it only tells you who is good at an initial reading! Remind the cast that some of the best actors are useless in a read-through.

It's good to have the M.D. there too so that she or he can play and sing the beginnings and ends of songs to give an idea of how they fit into the piece overall.

Auditions: remember to allow enough time …

Auditions

These can be fun! Throughout the initial activities above, you will have been sifting through the cast and forming ideas of who might be good at what. Set aside enough time to give everyone a fair chance, so consider auditioning in two stages on different occasions.

Stage one

This includes everyone and could be run along the lines indicated below, remembering to allow enough time for singing, dancing and acting. It's desirable for everybody on the artistic team to be present at the auditions.

Singing The M.D. can start by doing a general physical/vocal warm-up with everyone (see *Warm-ups*, page 30), then teaching part of a song and hearing the auditionees sing in groups of three or four, splitting down to twos as they gain confidence. Choose a short section of a song so that they can perform it from memory: this way you can see how they express the words and use their faces when singing. Ask anyone who wants to try for solos to sing the same song you have all worked on, but on their own. Be as encouraging as you can—it is quite an ordeal for some people to sing solo in public. Help them out with your voice or the piano if they begin to come unstuck, as it is unkind and entirely unnecessary to let them struggle. Try to have a répétiteur for this session. Make notes on vocal quality, range and stage presence. Also note any changing or broken voices among the males and difficulties with chest/head register with the girls (see *Register*, page 32).

Acting Short improvisations work well in auditions. For example, auditionee A plays the parent who has been waiting for his/her teenager B, to come home. B arrives at 3am. First time, play it with the parent at level 10 (highest tension) and child at level 0 (completely laid back), then play it again, reversing the levels. Or, be your pet (cat, rat, dog, fish) and in movement and words convey the most exciting thing that ever happened to you, in 30 seconds. For the second of these, ask the performer to make an entrance as the animal, deliver the monologue and make an exit.

Dance and movement It is crucial that you include some movement work with a strong creative element, which asks the performers to contribute ideas. Tableau work in large groups is a useful way of finding natural, expressive movers in the cast. For example, take a well-known story such as *Cinderella*, *Jack and the Beanstalk* or *The Pied Piper of Hamelin* and ask them to set up three picture moments from the story. Remind them they can include objects such as the beanstalk, the golden egg or animals. Ask them then to make an entrance in character, link each tableau with appropriate movement and make an exit from their final picture.

Many people are terrified of dancing, fearing they will 'make fools' of themselves. Men and boys often have the worst hang-ups, because dance for men is no longer part of our culture. Set a very short, simple dance sequence that can be taught to the group quickly. If possible, choreograph something that might be used in the show. For this part of the audition it would be very useful for someone with a lot of dance experience to teach the sequence so that you, as Choreographer, can watch and make notes.

Everything will proceed more quickly if you have a pianist present. If that is impossible, then choose some recorded music that can be played continuously, avoiding the problem of constantly winding back (use a CD rather than a tape). Split them into large groups and make sure you get a good idea of those who have reasonably good spatial awareness, physical coordination and a sense of timing and rhythm.

Stage two

Singing As before, get voices and bodies moving with a short warm-up. Make it fun and pacy so everyone can be as relaxed as possible. Choose two contrasting songs from the show and teach about 32 bars of each. Describe the age of the character, the accent required, the personality and the vocal range needed. Set the song in context and teach it with dramatic intent from the moment you start. You may have some fine concert singers auditioning who perhaps produce a lovely sound and line but cannot use the words well, change the timbre or 'characterize' the voice. Explain that they will be looked at as well as listened to, and must be able to perform their song with dramatic conviction. Don't forget some characters do not have to be able to sing particularly well: think of Professor Higgins in *My Fair Lady*!

Acting It is likely that you will want to hear a prepared piece at this stage. After Stage one, when you have selected those

Set a very short, simple dance sequence that can be taught to the group quickly

you want to see again for parts, give out a short piece of dialogue for two or three characters to learn before the audition day. At the recall audition, put the actors in groups to play it. Set the scene, give them a couple of minutes to set up, and then hear and watch each group's performance. Swap the roles around if you want to hear a particular actor playing a particular part. You might want to see how well they respond to direction as part of this exercise, for example. You will also know who has bothered to learn the parts; a good indicator for the future.

Dancing Concentrate on teaching set routines at this audition: make them more challenging, faster and longer than at the first audition. See auditionees perform in smaller groups and be more specific about style and expression. It is important at this stage to include dance that bears some relationship to the show. For example, if performing *Anything Goes* try Charleston (brittle, precise, animated, coordinated leg and hand gestures) or Busby Berkeley-style movement (positional, gestural, lots of formation work). For *Oklahoma* or *Seven Brides for Seven Brothers*, try an athletic version of American square dancing with lots of jumps, spins and lifts, working with a partner. If the show needs lots of dancers you will have called back quite a few people, fewer if the dance element is slight. Don't despair if you need a line-up of twenty tappers and you have only three: miracles can be worked with one or two basic steps in the back line and the flashy moves in front!

Understudies

Bear in mind during auditions that you will want to cast two people in each of the lead roles. Sometimes double-casting is used when there is nothing to choose between two contenders. It is good practice to run scenes with an understudy playing the part, partly to keep the understudy (or 'cover') on the ball, but also to allow the person playing the role to stand back and see how the scene works from the outside. Seeing a cover play a scene well can act as a spur to greater effort on the part of the first choice. It also means that the show can't be held to ransom by a sore throat or hangover!

The Band

Organizing and 'fixing' a band is a very lengthy affair involving many hours spent on the telephone, often to complete strangers! If you are new to the area or haven't needed a band before, here's where you might start:

❖ Local peripatetic instrumental teachers.
❖ County music service.
❖ Nearest music library.
❖ Local amateur operatic society.
❖ Heads of music at neighbouring secondary schools/colleges.

Don't be afraid to ask for recommendations from players and whether they expect a fee. You may have a large enough budget to pay peripatetic instrumental teachers or local semi-professional players. Alternatively you may be able to pay only a few but can find the rest from elsewhere, who will be happy to play for expenses only. Be very clear about who is receiving what so there is no room for misunderstanding. Don't forget parents, colleagues and students who may be around near holiday time. Who you finally ask will depend on:

❖ Budget.
❖ Difficulty of the band parts/ability of players.
❖ Availability of players.
❖ Reliability of players.

Playing in a pit band is not the same as playing in an orchestra. Parts often require changing instruments frequently (for example, moving from B♭ Clarinet to Alto Saxophone and back within 4 bars). Before you start on the phone calls, make sure you know exactly which instruments are needed. Information from the licensee often does not specify clearly whether the bass

Most Rodgers and Hammerstein-era musicals need players who can play a wide variety of wind instruments

is electric or acoustic, for example, so ask for a list of band parts early on. Most of the mainstream Rodgers and Hammerstein-era musicals need players who can play a wide variety of wind instruments:

Player 1: Flute/piccolo/clarinet/alto sax

These days it's almost impossible to find such a player and you may even have to get two covering the same part. If you cannot afford to hire the parts for more than a month, the players must be good sight-readers. All pit players must be able to follow very frequent tempo changes, be very patient, good-humoured and confident. If your players are less experienced and you want the parts for longer, there is a small extra charge.

When discussing rehearsal dates, make it clear that players are needed for every rehearsal when the band is called. With the relatively small number of rehearsals when all cast and band are together, it is vital that the instrumentalists understand this. Dates and times need to be written down clearly with the venue specified.

It is always a good idea to hold a band call three weeks or so before the performance. You then have time to sort out any technical or musical problems, set the tempi and establish an ensemble feel to the pit. You will have studied the score beforehand, but as most are cued piano scores, much may remain a mystery until you hear the band! Practise conducting the difficult tempo changes carefully, marking your score and being very clear about how many beats you are giving as preparation. If you are cutting sections of the music, check with the players that the instrument changes don't get in the way. Rehearse carefully the links in and out of cut sections as these can be a particular hazard.

Band players often seem very isolated in the dark, low, invisible world they inhabit! It is important to make them feel as much a part of the show as the actors on the stage. The whole business of putting on a musical is a team effort, so find ways to integrate these performers:

- Introduce the band to the cast at the earliest opportunity.
- Ask cast members to come to a band rehearsal and make tea/coffee for the players.
- Tell the band about the show/characters/songs/dance numbers: get them involved.
- Invite them to watch a rehearsal.
- Make sure you (and the cast) thank them for their hard work.
- Don't forget to invite them to any cast parties!

4   Teaching and staging a song

Before learning any of the songs, it is important to understand the musical style of the show. There are several considerations:

❖ Who was it written by? What else did they write?
❖ When is it set?
❖ Is it classical/mainstream/jazz/cabaret/rock/pop in style?
❖ What kind of orchestration does it have?
❖ Does the singing require an accent/dialect of any sort?

It may help to listen to a recording of your show, but only for a 'feel' of the music, not as a blueprint for the voices. Young singers need to make the part their own and not merely clone the original recording artist. In many cases, the freshness and sincerity of young voices can be more exciting than those on a commercial recording!

Teaching a song

The first vocal rehearsal will probably be seated; performers will be next to others singing the same vocal part (tenor, alto, etc.) and will be using vocal scores. It is important to learn the big chorus numbers first so the Choreographer can get started as soon as the singers are 'off the book'. This also creates a company feeling and makes everyone feel like a valued member of the cast. Try to divide your singers so that you have strong voices in each harmony part and seat them strategically. If you have a very small number of boys, seat them close to the piano. Then:

❖ Set the scene dramatically by describing where this song takes place and who the characters are.
❖ Play the number through to give the tempo, style and mood.
❖ Play it again whilst singing through the melody line, going for dialect straight away; don't be shy!
❖ Take the first section (around 8 to 16 bars) and note-bash each of the parts, with the singers repeating a phrase at a time. While one part is singing, ask the others to hum their parts so that they don't get bored; it reinforces their harmony part and begins to fix it in the memory.
❖ Try putting two of the parts together while the others hum or sing very quietly.

- Now try all parts together for this small section and help those who are struggling by singing with them or playing their part on the piano.
- Now try it standing up, without the copies and with expression and focus.

Learning in small chunks and memorizing as you go is the quickest way to get the music under your belt. The sooner you can be free of books the better, both for the Choreographer and for dramatic interpretation of the song.

It is helpful if a singing teacher can work with soloists from time to time, but very often teachers who are classically trained have not studied musical theatre and are not aware of the need for a change in vocal technique. They can, however, help tremendously with use of good breath support, clear diction and effective phrasing.

The voice needs to be as flexible as possible to aid character portrayal. Try the following either as a warm-up or as a prelude to teaching a particular song. Taking the first 4 bars of *Somewhere over the rainbow*, sing it as:

- Grand opera (find the 'Pavarotti feeling' in the diaphragm!).
- The witch in *The Wizard of Oz* (find the twang in the nose!).
- A cockney market trader.
- A Walt Disney princess.

These are all ways of 'colouring' the voice for a particular character. Notice how the voice can change, age, grow and shrink.

Decide how much of the number you are going to tackle in the first session (it may be two verses or verse and first chorus only) and move on to another song before concentration wavers and the situation becomes counter-productive. Check the harmony parts are still there at regular points; they have a strange habit of disappearing when singers move onto the stage!

Staging a song

Whoever undertakes this task, whether the Director or the Choreographer, they must adhere to some basic guidelines for safe practice:

- Make sure all performers are thoroughly warmed up, including late-comers.
- Check that anyone who has an injury is marking the movement or observing as appropriate.
- There should be adequate space for all to move freely and safely; encourage control and sensitivity to others when moving around.
  To practise particularly athletic moves, split the group if necessary.

❖ Make sure that footwear is suitable; a mixture of heavy outdoor shoes and jazz or ballet shoes in one room can lead to broken toes or painful kicks. Discourage the wearing of shoes with thick soles, unless of course this is part of the style of the piece. No one should be working in socks only as they will slip on almost any floor surface.

Make sure the footwear is suitable

❖ Ideally dance should take place on a sprung wooden floor. If your floor is less than ideal, do not ask for a high-impact activity that could cause injury.
❖ An experienced movement or dance teacher will know how to work with the correct body alignment. If the team doesn't include such a person, it would be helpful to bring in a local dance teacher or physical education specialist for guidance.
❖ Ensure that there are no potential hazards in the room, for example, chairs stacked so that they are unstable, or furniture with sharp corners protruding into the workspace. The room should be well-ventilated but not draughty or cold.

A good song will have a clear dramatic context. Before putting the song into its dramatic context within the piece, listen to a recording a lot to get the feel, mood and style. Consider the following questions:

- ❖ Which character is singing, and to whom?
- ❖ Is it a song that moves the action on, or is it reflective (a commentary on the action)?
- ❖ What is the stage setting?

Points to discuss with the M.D.:
- ❖ Is it a solo, duet or chorus number? If chorus, are there any solo lines or sections within it?
- ❖ If there are harmonies, does it affect grouping on the stage; for example, do all the middle parts need to be together?
- ❖ Are there any particular considerations about sound balance? Does the light-voiced soprano need to be near a float microphone, or does she have a radio one?
- ❖ Interpretation of the song: if you listen when the M.D. is teaching the song, you'll learn a good deal!

If the task of staging the song has fallen to you as the Choreographer, ask the Director:
- ❖ Does the song happen in the middle of a scene, or does it follow a scene change? Are the singers on, or do you have to bring them on during the introduction? If the latter, is the introduction long enough, or might you have to ask the M.D. to repeat a section? Is there scene change music?
- ❖ Where does the Director want the singers at the end of the song? Do they go straight into dialogue, exit, or freeze?
- ❖ What are the singers wearing and how will it affect their movement?
- ❖ Is there any set on stage? If so, where? Are any props required to be handled by the singers/movers?
- ❖ Find out if she/he has any particular thoughts about what needs to happen during the song, but try to avoid an over-prescriptive response. Try giving your own suggestions first.
- ❖ Ask if the Director will be present at the rehearsal; more likely than not she/he will seize the chance to do some small scene work elsewhere. Do make it clear that you would like the Director to see your work at the earliest opportunity so that any necessary adjustments can be made.

It's a good idea to start work with a song that involves as many people as possible. This will help everyone feel they have a role to play, and will encourage those who see themselves as 'only' chorus. If the schedule permits, workshop ideas with the cast first and ask them to contribute their thoughts. This can save time as it will give you a good idea of the strengths and weaknesses of the cast, as well as help you to get a feel for how they work as a group. Approaching the work in this way will help the performers to connect the movement and choreography with the drama and music of the piece, thus getting rid of the common misconception that choreography is just an opportunity for the dancers to show off.

Before you begin work on staging:

❖ Make sure the Stage Manager has marked up the performance space for you and given indications of entrances and the size and location of significant obstacles. If they take up too much space or break up the space in a particularly unhelpful configuration, be sure you have discussed this with the Designer before you start work.

❖ Find a small table and put your score, notes and script on it open at the right pages. You can easily lose your performers if you are constantly scrabbling through endless pages, as they will become unfocused, chatty and bored.

You can easily lose your performers if you're constantly scrabbling through endless pages …

❖ If you are working from a tape, either see if someone can operate it for you (dreams sometimes come true!) or note the tape counter numbers where various sections of the song begin. Alternatively, make a minidisc so that you can scan back and forth.

Let's take a particular song and see how it might be staged: 'Lullaby of Broadway' from *42nd Street* by Dubin and Warren. The show is set in the 1930s and the story line is basically about an unknown chorus girl who becomes a star. The song is lively and rhythmic, recreating the bustle of Broadway at night.

- Create characters: show-girls, taxi drivers, socialites, drunks, down-and-outs, men about town, young lovers, gangsters, waiters.
- Style: teach some basic dance steps from the time such as ballroom-dance holds and show-girl routines. Use some fashion pictures from the '30s to stimulate ideas about how to stand, sit, walk, gesticulate. Take in a bag of small props: scarves, cigarette-holders, canes, hats.
- Use any chairs or tables that are around to set up bar areas, or rostra to make a small stage area for a night club/bar, telephone booth, taxi stand, etc. Physical setting is very important in this kind of song and scene.
- Emphasize the energy of the song by moving people around and having different groups or individuals with their own set of actions and ideas happening at once. Contrast this with single-focus or unified action to allow the audience time to absorb what is going on.
- Set the opening and run it through a few times, asking for specific improvements each time. Work on through the song, always joining on the previously completed section until you get to the end. Don't worry if some of the moves are messy at this stage. It's important that you and the cast get a feel of the song as a whole and how it fits into the drama. You can work on detail later.
- Make careful notes soon after the rehearsal.

Some words of warning:
- Don't try to cram in too many images. The words of the song will do most of the work; you can't match visual image to word image because the visual needs more time to establish itself.
- Make sure there is empathy between the movement and the music in terms of rhythm, phrasing and breath control.
- Reassure the M.D. that you know the singing has nose-dived in quality from when they sang standing still. When action becomes the focus of the learning process, the singing will deteriorate. In the long run, have confidence that the singing will improve because movement ultimately energizes voices and informs interpretation.

It is always worthwhile to spend some time focusing on the voice, the body, communication and presentation skills before starting the rehearsal. It brings the company together, works towards a blend in the sound and generates a sense of purpose. The warm-up session gets performers breathing, loosened-up, moving, working together and focused as a group.

Physical warm-ups

Brains and bodies need to be mobilized and energized. It is very easy to pull muscles, so avoid stretching too early in a warm-up sequence.

Start on the spot, each person in their own space with enough distance between them and others to enable free movement. Stance or posture is important, so think of the soles of the feet as triangles and spread the weight evenly across the balls of the feet to their apex at the heels. Then:

- ❖ Emphasize the width of the upper chest; circle the shoulders backwards and forwards, adding the fingertips to the shoulders and drawing circles with the elbows to increase the opening of the chest (backwards), and the opening of shoulder blades (forwards).
- ❖ Visualize the shoulders and head as a coat hanger (the head is where the hook would be) and relax the shoulders down with heavy arms, whilst lifting the head from the point where the spine fits into the skull. Keep the chin parallel to the floor.
- ❖ Imagine a tail from the base of the spine going straight down to the floor, between the heels. Allow the pelvis to find its natural position by relaxing the seat muscles and loosening the knees. Gently shake out the arms and hands. Now you have an effective working stance.
- ❖ Leading with the head and arms, allow their weight to take the upper body forwards and down so that the spine curls while breathing out. Breathe in at the lowest point you can reach and then unroll the spine back up on an out-breath until the body is upright once more. Take care to realign the pelvis and relax the shoulders, with the head coming up last. Repeat four times.
- ❖ Shake out hands, wrists, elbows, shoulders, middles, hips, knees, ankles, feet, heads until the whole body is like one big jelly.
- ❖ Swing the arms forward and back, bending the knees as the arms swing through the lowest point of the arc and straightening as they rebound up and forwards, or back. Gradually increase the size of the swing, allowing

the spine to curl forwards as the arms swing down. On reaching the top of the arc lift the arms above the head, reaching for the ceiling before the momentum swings you back down.

❖ Perform four or eight large body swings, bearing in mind that the smaller the body, the faster the swing! Vary the swings by adding in arm circles, changing the direction of the movement, and adding simple travelling steps. Music with a waltz rhythm will help the group to feel the movement.

❖ Regain a working stance and draw figures of eight with your nose in front, then above, to the sides and downwards. Vary the size and speed, and be aware of the movement in the muscles of your neck. Finish by relaxing the head forward and gently shaking it as if saying 'no'.

❖ Walk anywhere in the space, moving around other people and looking for spaces. Change direction either on a signal, or by basing the floor pattern on a series of curving lines. Let your body go with the curve and make eye contact with others. Play with the speed of the walk. Give it a dramatic focus: late, too early, nervous, confident; or a situation: running for a bus, jogging in the park, and so on.

Before you hand over the group to the M.D. make sure they are energized and not exhausted!

Vocal health

Some of these tips may seem obvious, but it is useful to keep them in mind:

❖ Encourage singers to bring drinking water to rehearsals (but not to share bottles!).

❖ Don't let anyone sing on a sore throat.

❖ Make sure the room is well ventilated.

❖ Check posture for signs of straining.

❖ If you have a large band, amplify the singers; don't let them shout or strain to be heard.

❖ If a young singer has a recurrent problem with sore throats, persuade them to see a doctor; glandular fever is a common cause and if that is the case they should not be singing.

Make sure the room is well ventilated

❖ Medicated throat sweets should be avoided; natural/glycerine pastilles are just as effective and do not mask the pain that is nature's warning signal.

❖ If possible, have understudies for the principal parts.

Register

A common problem with girls is that they tend to use only their chest register when singing pop or musical theatre songs. If you try singing up a scale from the A below middle C and stay resolutely in chest register, you will feel the voice getting tighter as it rises, until it goes through a kind of gear change into head voice. This usually occurs around the G/A area above middle C; there is an immediate change of tone and often loss of volume and energy in the sound.

Most pop songs work best in the chest register, which is fine if the song sits happily in the lower/middle part of this range. However, if you use this voice most of the time, the upper register or head voice will become very weak and a noticeable mismatch between the two sounds will develop. It is a very uncomfortable feeling to sing across this break and many girls simply don't know how to handle it. A classic example of the problem occurs in the song 'As long as he needs me' from *Oliver*. Everything is going smoothly in chest register until the last verse when the song modulates up a semitone. In nearly every case the poor soloist cannot hit the final 'needs' in the chest voice, and either the note breaks and yodels or a tiny, breathy, weak note appears in the head voice. What are the solutions?

- ❖ Always warm up the whole voice, not just the lower end.
- ❖ Awareness of technique: understand girls' voices and decide where and when they may need to change registers.
- ❖ Make sure that girls can access their head voice easily and with good support.
- ❖ Never ask them to sing louder in the chest register. Instead, amplify if necessary.
- ❖ Try to find a show that has a wide vocal range.

Vocal warm-ups

Everyone has now stretched, loosened up and worked on posture. This is vital for effective and safe use of the voice. Before getting going vocally, check that the weight is on both feet, the knees are loose and not locked, and shoulders and hands are relaxed. Think about breathing; we all do it or we wouldn't be here!

- ❖ Blow out all the breath in the body, then breathe in deeply and naturally without letting the shoulders lift.
- ❖ Bend forward with hands out in front and repeat, feeling the breath go into the back on the inhalation.

+ Now repeat standing up straight and really notice the breath filling the whole of the middle part of the body, front and back (it is important to understand that the diaphragm is where the support for the voice comes from).
+ This time, after the inhalation, hum a comfortable note for a count of four (M.D. click the beat), making sure the lungs have been completely emptied by the last beat.
+ Change to an open vowel, 'eee', 'ooh' or 'ah', and increase the length of the sound to eight beats then sixteen, feeling the control and pace of the exhalation.

Warm up some of the important face muscles:
+ Make a small face (screw up all the muscles into the middle). On a clap, make the face as big as possible (wide open mouth, eyebrows lifted).
+ Place fingers on the 'hinge' of the jaw and feel the degree of movement when opening and closing the mouth.
+ Pretend to be chewing gum with an open mouth, loudly and quickly; feel those lips, tongue and jaw wake up.

Show how you feel as a character: sad, proud, angry, surprised, confused, scared, shocked, etc. This involves the whole face as well as the body, so think big! It sometimes helps if company members focus on each other as well as on the 'audience'.

For good articulation, try a couple of tongue-twisters or nonsense words to get the lips/tongue/jaw moving well:
+ Try the words in a whisper.
+ Mouth them with no breath.
+ Try them with an American accent (find the 'twang' in the sound).
+ Try them as different characters from the show you are performing.

A good eye-line and focused attention are probably the most vital communication tools. This warm-up gets everyone moving together and generates a feeling of alertness. Always check there is energy in the face and life in the eyes.

+ Choose three focal points in the space facing the 'audience': one stage left (the performers' left) called focus 1; one central, focus 2; one stage right (the performers' right), focus 3.
+ On a click of the fingers, everyone takes focus 1 with the head, eyes and full attention.

❖ Next click go to focus 2, then click to focus 3.

❖ Stay on each focus for different lengths of time to challenge the concentration!

Before getting the voice moving gently and safely, check that posture is still good (weight, knees and shoulders). Remind performers of the support around the diaphragm.

❖ Hum a gentle siren from low to high and back down again (always check eyebrows are helping at the upper end!).

❖ Change this to an open 'ah', ensuring no chins rise and that shoulders and hands are still relaxed.

❖ Look at focus 1 and imagine you can see a long-lost friend across a crowded supermarket; throw your arm and voice across three aisles with a 'yoo-hoo' at the top of your range. Feel your voice in your boots as you then say 'it's me!' at your lowest pitch. This exercise is wonderful for finding high notes in a safe, quasi-operatic style. It makes everyone laugh and helps boys with changing voices to access their falsetto. If ever you have a problem in getting a good sound in the higher sections, try singing a quick 'yoo-hoo' to place the voice safely and with rounded tone.

Warm-ups should be challenging, thoughtful, effective and, above all, fun! The company should now be alert, focused, working together and ready to begin rehearsing.

In *Getting going*, we offered some ideas about ways in which rehearsals can be approached to ease the cast's way into the show and to explore aspects such as style, character, story and context. This preparatory work will save a lot of time when you come to the process of creating the show.

Practicalities

❖ Make sure the room looks ready for work: enlist the help of early birds to organize the space. If you have any control over it, check the temperature and ventilation.

❖ Include a good physical and vocal warm-up. Encourage people to wear comfortable clothes in which they can move easily, and shoes with soft soles. If they need specific shoes or skirts for character or dance work, they should bring them to put on when required.

❖ Start and finish on time. Starting a rehearsal late, or working later than scheduled, will not encourage cast punctuality or goodwill.

❖ Take a short break for drinks and gossip. Parish notices can be made at this point, as well as calls for the next rehearsal (nobody will listen at the end).

❖ Don't call people for rehearsal if you are not going to use them. Instead, you might want to call principals early and work with them before the others arrive, or finish some people earlier than others.

❖ Rehearsals can be very tiring. Try to limit the amount of new moves, etc., to be absorbed in any one session, to avoid loss of concentration in the cast; for example, balance blocking new moves with repetition of previously blocked sections.

❖ Well-run rehearsals should be satisfying, productive and disciplined. When working with young people, introduce a system for signalling a run of a song or a scene. 'Stand by' is a useful phrase; it means go to the right place, stop chatting, and find focus and concentration. When you get into the theatre, any work you have done on cast discipline during rehearsals will pay off. It is essential that they understand the need for quiet backstage at all times. Some people need to concentrate and be quiet before they go on stage; others should respect this need.

❖ At the start of rehearsals, set a date by which all lines must be learned, and stick to it!

REHEARSAL SCHEDULE

When		Who/What	Why
Week 0		Director Choreographer Designer	Preliminary discussions so that a model of the set and costume sketches can be presented at the meeting in week 1
Week 1	Monday	Director Set designer Costume designer Lighting designer Choreographer	Meeting to finalize design and production ideas
	Thursday	All production, technical and artistic staff	Meeting to OK the schedule and clarify matters relating to individual areas of responsibility
Week 2	Monday Thursday	Stage one auditions Stage two auditions	To cast the show and allocate roles. Check availability for Easter vacation rehearsals
Week 3	Monday	Rehearsals start	Full company call for read-through and workshops
Weeks 4–8		Rehearsals continue	
Week 9		4-day intensive rehearsal period	NB Wardrobe in and costume-fittings as cast available; all props to be available; run scene change rehearsal on final day with set if available, or substitute
Week 10	Monday	All required	First run (stagger) of Act 1 Running repairs to Act 1
Week 11	Monday	All required	First run (stagger) of Act 2 Running repairs to Act 2
Week 12	Monday	All required	Run Acts 1 and 2 in costume as far as possible for lighting designer
	Thursday		Running repairs
Week 13 (Pre-production week)	Sunday Monday Tuesday Thursday	All required	Set on stage Act 1 run (photos) Act 2 run (photos) Run both Acts in costume

Overall schedule

This defines what is to be included in order to arrive at the point of performance in a state of readiness. Plan each rehearsal, keeping in mind what should have been achieved by the end of it.

❖ Share out time spent on singing, dancing and dialogue. Make best use of time by giving soloists a session with the M.D. while the Director and/or Choreographer work with ensemble sections.

❖ Estimate when you might be able to stagger through (see page 42) then run Act One, Act Two and then the whole show.

❖ Work out the schedule backwards from the get-out following the final show. Write down all show dates and times, dress rehearsals and technical rehearsals, and include the calls for band, cast and crew (don't forget to schedule in a photo call). A sample production schedule can be found on page 38.

From page to stage

These rehearsals are where the artistic team, technical team and the performers put the show together. Working with the cast and the other members of the artistic team, the Director blocks the action. This creates a physical realization of what is written in the script and score, piecing together individual scenes to achieve continuity and coherence.

The Stage Manager will call or cue the show using 'the book' as the blueprint for the production. The cast may need to be reminded that they must learn their own moves and cues as well as lines, songs and music. The Stage Manager will be able to remind them in the rehearsal room, but once in the theatre they will need to be self-sufficient.

Blocking

It is at the point where blocking begins that the Stage Manager's mark-up of the stage space within the rehearsal space becomes very important. To create the drama on stage, the Director works with the actors on:

❖ Delivery of lines and dialogue, i.e. sense (who they are talking to, is there a sub-text and if so, how it is revealed), clarity and audibility.

❖ Placing of scenery, furniture, props, actors.

❖ Focus.

❖ Specific character development.

❖ Significance of particular incidents depicted in the scene.

❖ Continuity: what led into the scene and how it leads into the next action.

❖ Placing entrances and exits.

PRODUCTION SCHEDULE

Date	Times	What	Who	Where
Friday 11 June	15:30–23:30	Get-in	All crew and volunteers	Theatre NB must clear building by 00:00
Saturday 12 June	09:00–12:00	Plotting of lights	LX (lighting) operator, Designer, Stage Manager, Director	Theatre
	10:00–12:30	Band rehearsal	M.D. and soloists as called	Rehearsal Room
	13:30–15:00	Sitzprobe	Cast and band	Rehearsal Room
	13:30–15:00	Technical work	Stage Manager, Crew, LX	Theatre
	15:30–18:00	Sound balance	Cast and band	Theatre
	19:00–21:30	Technical rehearsal of Act 1 (piano)	Cast, crew and production team	Theatre
Sunday 13 June	09:30–10:30	Technical time on stage	Stage Manager and crew	Theatre
	09:30	Cast into costume	Costume designer and Wardrobe	Dressing Rooms
		Physical/vocal warm-up	Choreographer and M.D.	Rehearsal Room
	10:30–12:30	Technical rehearsal of Act 2 (piano)	All cast and crew	Theatre
	13:30–16:00	Technical rehearsal of Act 1 and 2 in costume	Cast, crew and band	Theatre
	16:00	Crew notes	Director	Theatre
	16:00	Band notes	M.D.	Rehearsal Room
	16:30	Cast notes	Director, Choreographer and M.D.	Theatre
	17:30	Vocal warm-up	M.D.	
	17:45	Cast into costume and microphones fitted	Wardrobe	Dressing Rooms/ Rehearsal Room
	18:15	Dress Rehearsal		Theatre
	20:45	Crew notes	Director	Theatre
	21:00	Cast notes	Director, Choreographer and M.D.	Theatre
	21:30	Finish		
Monday 14 June	18:00	Warm up cast	M.D. and Choreographer	Rehearsal Room
	18:30	Cast to wardrobe and microphones fitted		Dressing Rooms/ Rehearsal Room
	19:00	Band call		
	19:15	Focus warm-up	Director	Rehearsal Room
	19:30	Performance 1 NB notes to be given at 18:00 on Tuesday 15 June		Theatre

Getting actors off the book, i.e. lines learned, as early as possible is essential. Once a scene is blocked, run back over it and make any adjustments needed; it is difficult to change moves once they have begun to be absorbed by the performers. It is also important to develop a sense of character in early rehearsals or workshops (see page 17), so that when blocking begins the actors can understand how to react and interact with others. They will then understand the motivation for certain moves or responses and can contribute their own ideas, allowing each character to grow through the rehearsal period. Here are some practicalities to bear in mind:

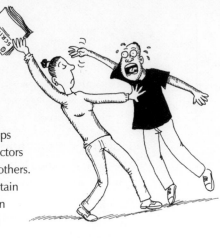

Getting actors 'off the book' is essential …

❖ Don't wait for actual props and furniture to materialize; improvise with anything around. Chairs are useful and can be used as beds, tables, rocks, trees, walls, etc.

❖ Block scene changes as you go, giving individual cast members jobs to do, and write them down. They won't forget they have a solo, but they will forget to take off the basket of logs while denying it was ever their responsibility!

❖ Transitions between scenes need to be thought out. Use blackouts sparingly: although useful for triggering audience applause (such as following a big musical number with a flamboyant finish), too many can fracture continuity and break audience concentration.

Don't wait for actual props to materialize: improvise!

- Some shows call for a continuity of physical location, for example, the school is always up-stage left (i.e., the back of the stage on the actors' left).
- Bear in mind audience sight lines. Extreme USL and USR may be out of view of some audience members, so avoid setting crucial action where it might be missed.

Final rehearsals and performance

The get-in and fit-up is the point at which the school, village hall or municipal, general-purpose performance space is transformed into your theatre. Make sure you have enough volunteers lined up to help bring in staging, lighting equipment, furniture, props and costumes. Remember that:

- Lights need rigging and focusing.
- Sound equipment has to be set up.
- Staging has to be erected and made safe.
- Costumes need unpacking, ironing and hanging on rails.
- The set needs to be hung or possibly flown (i.e. raised up and down on a pulley operated by one of the stage crew known as the Flyman), assembled and placed.
- Off-stage storage needs to be determined, including a props table set out and labelled.

Lighting

Once blocking has taken place, the lighting design will have been agreed by the Director and Lighting Designer. Earlier discussions will have determined what special lighting effects might be needed, such as follow spots or projections onto the cyclorama, backcloth or wall.

The main task for any lighting design is to illuminate the action on stage, so initially it is a good idea to concentrate on achieving two or three basic lighting states, or overall stage cover, with different moods. A warm state can be achieved with mainly yellows and golds with a small amount of orange, and a cold state with steel blue and

Poorly positioned stage lights can dazzle an audience

some slightly stronger blues. White light, i.e. no colour, will give a stark, harsh effect. Light can also be used to highlight dramatic action, feature a particular performer, enhance the plasticity of dancing bodies by lighting from the sides of the stage, create silhouettes with back lighting, feature a full moon or a forest fire on the backdrop and so on.

Plotting the lighting means the Director and the Lighting Designer working together to achieve the sequence of lighting changes for the show, from the start when the house lights dim, to the end. Many lighting boards are computerized, so lights, their levels and the timings of changes can be put into the board to be cued by the Stage Manager during performances. It is useful during the plotting to have some people around so you can try some lighting on bodies, rather than lighting the stage floor.

Band lights are there to enable the players to read their music, but they, and poorly positioned stage lights, can also dazzle the audience. Adjusting the angles of any lights and placing dark blue gels over the band lights will help to reduce the problem.

Sound

It is important to use the best sound system you can afford so that voices can be heard without distortion, and the sound is enhanced rather than amplified. If the budget is small, consider using float microphones instead of radio microphones and position performers accordingly. Rock musicals have to be extensively amplified as electric keyboards and guitars easily drown the singer, but some musicals are lightly scored and if your band players are experienced and carefully situated, you may get away with a basic sound system.

Plan your sound with the Sound Engineer in good time, so that any problems may be solved before you get into the theatre space. Decide on any sound effects needed and plot exactly when they occur (some are 'ambient sound' to set the scene, for example, birdsong; others are more precise, for example, a door shutting). If there are many solo lines in a number, soloists may be able to sing into another singer's radio microphone. This can work very well but needs careful blocking. Singers who use radio microphones need to have them preset before they make up; they can then be disguised, carefully avoiding the microphone head. The battery pack is usually fixed to a belt but some soloists may have to wear a special pouch underneath their costume if it is tight-fitting or very revealing!

Technical rehearsals

These are mainly for the lighting, sound and stage crews to get their act together. It can be a very useful to include a technical run of the show with the cast as well, but do not allow artistic aspects to take precedence over technical, although it is possible to 'tweak' artistically as the technical rehearsal progresses. Do as much organization and running of technical elements as you can before the get-in. The planning of the final part of your pre-production schedule needs to be done very carefully, and should include:

Scene change rehearsal It is likely that both the cast and stage management will be involved in moving props or set between scenes, so this rehearsal also allows concentration on potentially hazardous moments when large pieces of set are being flown in and out. Ideally the Stage Manager should run this rehearsal in sequence, working with the Director. It is essential that all tasks are listed with the name of the actor noted. All stage management will also be involved; ensure they know they need to wear black clothes and quiet shoes for the dress rehearsal and shows.

Stagger through This is a stopping run of the show. The purpose is to solve any artistic and technical difficulties prior to the full technical rehearsal and should be run in the rehearsal space, helping towards economical use of theatre time. It is also the first time all the elements of the show will have been put together—songs, choreography, dialogue—and will enable the Director and artistic team to gain a sense of whether:

❖ The story is being told.
❖ The geography of the set is working.
❖ The pacing of the show as a whole is going in the right direction; are there scenes that feel as though they are dragging on, or zipping through too fast for the drama to be clear?

Sound check Allow enough time to balance the sound between singers and band, particularly if singers are using radio microphones.

Technical on-stage work The crew will need time to prepare for the smooth running of the show. It is essential to schedule time for them to work on-stage unhampered by cast.

Final technical rehearsal Run the whole show, taking a timed break for an interval if there is one. Stop only for major technical problems, which must be solved immediately by going back. The Stage Manager will call the show, i.e. cue lighting and effects, from backstage and deliver the cues in two stages: standby and go. The Stage Manager will also make sure that scene changes are carried out at the right time by the backstage crew and cast.

It is essential that the sequence of events leading up to the start of the show is carefully worked out and rehearsed. Imagine the scene: the audience is seated, house lights go down and nothing happens. Nobody has cued the M.D. who isn't sure whether or not to begin, just in case there is a backstage problem that she/he doesn't know about …

Give the crew notes immediately after the run while the cast takes a break. Then allow technical time on stage to solve the inevitable problems of doors that won't close or squeaky truck wheels before you proceed to the next stage.

Dress rehearsal Dress rehearsals are replicas in every respect of the performances. It is often useful to have in an invited audience; this will help the cast to allow time for audience responses such as laughs, applause, etc. Decide beforehand when and where you and other artistic staff will give notes on the dress rehearsal and performances to the cast, band and crew.

Notes
Ask the cast to bring a small notebook with them to write down any comments that particularly apply to them. Give notes as soon as you feel the cast and production are ready. By the time you are running Acts through, notes should feature. Always make time for notes sessions following the dress rehearsals and performances, except the last one!

Give notes on the previous performance before the warm-up for the next one.

Stop only for major technical problems

- The aim of notes is to enable performers and technical crew to maintain the standard and even improve upon the performances. Notes sessions should be snappy, specific and, where, possible fun. Balance criticism with praise. The Choreographer and M.D. will want to contribute.
- Impress on the cast that they should listen to comments made, not attempt to allocate blame elsewhere, give excuses or comment. Build in a short time at the end of a notes session where you will take questions, but emphasize that these should be relevant to others, not just the individual.
- Make sure the ensemble receives due attention; they are often astonished that someone notices what they do!
- If possible, run anything that needs to be sorted out with regard to script or moves. Dance steps can be included in the warm-up, which is far more effective than a discussion.

Curtain calls

These must be rehearsed, otherwise all your hard work will end in chaos. Remember that adrenalin runs high at the end of a show and the cast will need to contain their excitement until they are out of the public eye and hearing! The Last Night can be an excuse for relaxing concentration, playing tricks and generally spoiling the last performance. An after-show party might encourage private rather than public exuberance. Similarly, it will provide an opportunity for presentations and thanks, which do not belong in the public arena.

Decide on the line-up and make sure that everyone can see someone placed centre front. Ask that person to lead the bows by taking a deep breath as a preparation, lifting the head back slightly and then bowing; just hold the arms relaxed at the sides, avoiding the stomach clutch! The others need to synchronize their movement with the leader, who uses the breath as a visual preparation.

Traditionally the Stage Manager decides on whether or not a second curtain call is justified, so be sure both the S.M. and the cast are clear about the procedure. Give the number of bows, say two, to the audience, indicate the M.D. who will include the band, one more to the audience, and lights down. Sometimes curtain calls will be choreographed to fit in with the feel of the show, for example, traditional pantomime curtain calls. The sombre finish of a show such as *West Side Story* requires very different handling. Remind the cast that the bows are allowing them to acknowledge the audience's appreciation and that they can look pleased!

There are several important legal and safety requirements when putting on a show. Someone needs to check the paperwork and take responsibility for ensuring nothing is overlooked. With so many things to think about in the rehearsal period, they can easily be forgotten. Here are a few vital points:

❖ Public Liability Insurance.
❖ License agreement with publisher of show (including wording of publicity material).
❖ Box Office receipts and payment of royalties.

Fire regulations
Make sure you know exactly how many people you are allowed to seat in the audience and how the chairs should be attached to each other. Fire exits must be clearly marked and fire extinguishers up to date and accessible. Keep aisles clear at all times.

First aid
It is advisable to have two people with first aid qualifications at each performance; try asking St. John's Ambulance if they can supply attendants for you. Check that your venue has a first aid kit available and handy. Ice-packs should be available for on-stage sprains and bruises.

Safety
If you are getting in temporary raised seating for the audience, then safety rails must be fitted according to regulations. All cables and leads must be taped to the floor and covered, and remember to use safety chains on lanterns. Warn audiences of any use of strobe lighting.

The cast and crew must be given an orientation session in the theatre by someone familiar with the building and its layout. It is essential to show exit routes and allow the cast to explore the backstage area under the supervision of the Stage Manager. Remember that there should be an appropriate level of light in the wings, above doorways on and off stage, and that changes of floor level should be marked with white paint or tape. If scenery is being flown in and out, be careful to warn the cast so that they are aware of the danger, and avoid setting exits and entrances in the vicinity.

Scripts, scores and band parts

You will have paid a deposit on the hire of the above. Try to keep a record of who has which script (number them lightly in pencil) and make sure they are returned in good time the week of the show. Band parts must have all markings rubbed out before they are returned (issue players with erasers at the last performance; it would take one person weeks to do it all!) and remember to keep the original packing material to send it all back!

Suggested reading

Barker, Clive. *Theatre Games* (Methuen Publishing Ltd, 1977)
Bond, Daniel. *Stage Management* (A & C Black Ltd, 1997)
Green, Stanley. *Encyclopaedia of the Musical Theatre* (Dodd, Mead & Co., 1976)
Jackson, Sheila. *More Costumes for the Stage* (Herbert Press, 1998)
Pickering, Kenneth & Sunderland, Margot. *Choreographing the Stage Musical* (J. Garnet Miller, 1989)
Read, Francis. *Stage Lighting* (A & C Black Ltd, 1992)
Theodorou, Michael. *Ideas that work in Drama* (Nelson Thornes, 1990)
White, Matthew. *Staging a Musical* (A & C Black Ltd, 1999)

Song resources for devised work

Marsh, Lin. *Metropolis* (Faber Music)
Marsh, Lin. *Songscape* (Faber Music)
Marsh, Lin. *Along Came Man* (Piper Publications)
Marsh, Lin. *Song of the Earth* (Piper Publications)
Rose, Peter & Conlon, Anne. *Ocean World* (Weinberger)
Rose, Peter & Conlon, Anne. *Arabica* (Weinberger)

Publishers of musicals

Alfred A. Kalmus Ltd/Universal Edition London. Tel 0800 525566. retail@mdsmusic.co.uk
Alfred Publishing Co. (UK) Ltd. Tel 01279 828960. Fax 01279 828961.
music@alfredpublishing.demon.co.uk
Alison Hedger Children's Music. Tel/Fax 01425 274993. alison_hedger@lineone.net
Ariel Music. Tel 01295 780679. Fax 01295 788630. jane@arielmusic.co.uk
A & C Black (Publishers) Ltd. Tel 01480 212666. Fax 01480 405014. sales@acblack.com
Boosey & Hawkes Music Publishers Ltd. Tel 020 7580 2060. www.boosey.com
Cramer Music. Tel 020 7240 1612. Fax 020 7240 2639
Dramatic Lines Publishers. Tel 0800 5429570. Fax 020 8296 9503. Orders@dramaticlines.co.uk.
www.dramaticlines.co.uk
Eschenbach Editions. Tel 0131 667 3633. eschenbach@caritas-music.co.uk.
www.caritas-music.co.uk
J. Garnet Miller. Tel/Fax 01684 540154
Josef Weinberger Ltd. Tel 020 7580 2827. Fax 020 7436 9616. generalinfo@jwmail.co.uk.
www.josef-weinberger.com
Lindsay Music. Tel 01767 316521. Fax 01767 317221. sales@lindsaymusic.co.uk.
www.lindsaymusic.co.uk
Magical Musicals Limited. Tel/Fax 01268 542531. info@magicalmusicals.co.uk
Music Sales Ltd. *Publishers and distributors of a wide range and varied selection of musicals and
shows by Golden Apple, Chester, Shawnee Press, Novello, Hal Leonard (Williamson), Really
Useful Group and Youngsong.* Tel 01284 773666. Fax 01284 702592.
music@musicsales.co.uk. www.musicroom.com
Pavilion Music. Tel 01273 689657. Pavilion.music@virgin.net
Piper Publications. Tel 01465 821377. www.piperpublications.co.uk
The Really Useful Group Ltd. Tel 020 7240 0880. Fax 020 7240 1204.
robinsond@reallyuseful.co.uk. www.reallyuseful.com
Samuel French Ltd. Tel 020 7387 9373. Fax 020 7387 2161. theatre@samuelfrench-london.co.uk
Sound Music. Tel 01904 410298. Fax 01904 421109
Sweet 'n' Sour Songs Ltd. Tel 020 7282 7767. Fax 020 7383 3020
Tyne Music. Tel/Fax 0191 232 2479. tynemusic@usa.net. www.tynemusic.co.uk
Warner/Chappell Music Ltd. Tel 020 8563 5887. Fax 020 8563 5801